Nicholas Patrick Wiseman

The Religious and Social Position of Catholics in England

An Address Delivered to the Catholic Congress of Malines, August 21,

1863

Nicholas Patrick Wiseman

The Religious and Social Position of Catholics in England
An Address Delivered to the Catholic Congress of Malines, August 21, 1863

ISBN/EAN: 9783337130688

Printed in Europe, USA, Canada, Australia, Japan

Cover: Foto ©Lupo / pixelio.de

More available books at **www.hansebooks.com**

THE

RELIGIOUS AND SOCIAL POSITION

OF

CATHOLICS IN ENGLAND.

—

———

AN ADDRESS

DELIVERED TO

THE CATHOLIC CONGRESS OF MALINES,

AUGUST 21, 1863.

BY H. E. CARDINAL WISEMAN.

Translated from the French.

DUBLIN:
JAMES DUFFY, 15, WELLINGTON-QUAY, AND
22, PATERNOSTER-ROW, LONDON.
1864.

ONE of the subjects proposed to be treated in the great " Catholic Congress," held at Malines, in the month of August last, was the situation of Catholics in different countries.

England, so variously and pleasingly allied with Belgium, could not fail to take a prominent place in this class of topics; and it naturally fell to the author of this Address to appear as the representative of English Catholics.

The speech, as taken down by the shorthand writers for the *Compte-rendu* of the meeting, has been corrected, and in some places expanded; since, though it occupied a long time in delivery, the speaker found it necessary to compress his thoughts occasionally. Delay in publication has been caused by waiting for the French proofs, and by ill health.

London, December 11*th,* 1863.

THE RELIGIOUS AND SOCIAL POSITION

CATHOLICS IN ENGLAND.

My Lord Cardinal, my Lords and Gentlemen,

If practised and accomplished orators have felt constrained to express to you the emotion excited within them, on standing in the presence of this immense and majestic assembly, with what apprehension must I, a stranger (so far as a Catholic can be a stranger in the midst of Catholics), in feeble health, and speaking a language not my own, approach the task of treating, before you, a subject no less vast than delicate. I can assure you that in doing so I fear to appear rash and even presumptuous. One thing, however, reassures me : I do not come here as an orator, nor do I aspire to win the palm of eloquence. I am a simple reporter, who comes with a few plain figures to occupy your attention, or, it may be to weary you, for a few moments. I am about simply to relate to you facts which I believe to be worthy of the interest and sympathy of all Catholics ; and the kind reception which you have already given me assures me of your patient indulgence.

I have undertaken to speak to you of the religious, civil, and social condition of the Catholics of England. But, before I enter upon my subject, permit me to say that, far from coming here to teach, I am come, on the contrary, to learn and to admire. Whenever I visit Belgium, as I occasionally do, I am amazed at the sight of all the beautiful and useful works which distinguish this country, and render it great, notwithstanding the narrowness of its territory. I must even confess that I am somewhat humbled for my country, although I cease not to thank God for· what He is doing there for His Church.

When I contemplate your magnificent cathedrals, and the ceremonies continually celebrated within them ; when I look at the episcopate of your country, at those illustrious prelates, so exemplary for their piety, their devotedness, and their zeal ; when I consider this numerous body of clergy, so indefatigable in their ministry and in their defence of religion, labouring indefatigably, day and night, for the welfare of their flocks ; when, lastly, I behold this marvellous assembly of Belgian Catholics, both laymen and ecclesiastics, united for an object which is truly sublime, I confess that I feel overwhelmed by the noble and consoling spectacle of Catholic Belgium, especially at this moment, which seems to put the finishing stroke to her religious glory.

You are aware, gentlemen, that Catholicism in England is in a progressive state. This is a truth not only recognised by all the members of the Catholic Church, but admitted also by those who do not belong to her. Everybody in England seems to acknowledge that Catholicism is daily gaining ground upon Protestantism. In fact, this admission is the ground of many important proceedings on the part of our religious adversaries. Gigantic societies and institutions are founded for the avowed purpose of impeding our growth ; and speeches in public assemblies sound the alarm, and strive to excite the national mind by this topic. Still a few facts will enable you better to judge of the importance of this progress, and these facts will consist of simple statistics carefully framed. There is no eloquence more conclusive, or more persuasive, than that of figures, on a subject like this ; and all fear of exaggeration will be thus entirely avoided.

We may fix on three epochs, each of which

marks the date of a step in the progress of English Catholicism :—

The first is the Civil Emancipation of Catholics, the commencement for them of a great material and social advancement. The second, ten years later, is marked by the Extension of the Episcopate, which led to a great religious development. After the same interval comes the third epoch, indelibly characterised by the Creation of a Hierarchy, and a complete ecclesiastical organization in England.

In 1829 the first of these events took place in England, one which most powerfully contributed to the progress of Catholicism—the Civil Emancipation of Catholics. The measure for it passed on the 23rd of April, 1829. By it Catholics obtained a remarkable augmentation of their social privileges. The oppressive laws, those especially which barred their entrance into the two Houses of Parliament, and the high functions of the magistracy and the government, were definitely abolished. We may, therefore, say that, since that moment, Catholics have been legally placed on an equality with Protestants. But, practically, various restrictions and humiliations still remained which rendered the position of Catholics painful, and the abolition of which is still the object of our continual endeavours.

The year 1829 was to us what the egress from the catacombs was to the early Christians. Previous to that date Catholics had been almost afraid to show themselves openly—they concealed the poor chapels which they built, not only by placing them in obscure corners and ill-inhabited quarters, but by disguising them under the uncomely appearance of dissenting meeting-houses. Anti-Catholic feeling was sometimes so violent, that I remember a town where a priest, having ventured to cause a cross to be traced in the plaster on the façade of a little chapel which he was building, was warned by the mayor, that he could not be answerable for the safety of the building unless that sacred emblem were effaced. So intense there was the hatred of the Catholic name.

One circumstance which contributed to forward the Act of Emancipation, was the fact that Catholics, being assured of the protection of the State, had already begun to assume some courage, and to show themselves more boldly in the face of their enemies in asserting their rights as fellow-subjects. Still, it must be confessed, that it has been especially since the year 1829 that the exterior expansion of Catholicism has been most visibly manifested.

Ten years later, on the 30th of July, 1840, Pope

Gregory XVI. doubled the number of Bishops, still, however, preserving the form of government by Vicars Apostolic.   This was, indeed, an immense step ; for by this measure the natural action of the Episcopate was enabled to develop itself more widely and more energetically in England ; and you will presently see how fruitful in results that action has been.

Lastly, in 1850, our Holy Father, Pius IX., granted to England its present Episcopal Hierarchy, and nominated an Archbishop and twelve Bishops to compose it.   This measure has not only contributed to diffuse the Episcopal action still more widely over England, but may be said to have bestowed a new life on Catholicism, by creating a new form of existence for our Church.

We may say, gentlemen, that this gradual development of the English Episcopate was a providential dealing.   For, at an earlier period, we should not have known what to do with our present privileges, and with Hierarchichal organization, such as we now enjoy.   We should not even have possessed the material means necessary to set in motion, or to second the powers, wherewith the Holy See has since endowed us.

Permit me to lay before you, in figures, a simple

view of the effect produced by these gradual measures.

The census of the population of England gives the following numbers of its inhabitants :—

For the year 1831,	...	13,896,797
„ 1841,	...	15,914,148
„ 1851,	...	17,927,609
„ 1861,	...	20,066,224

that is, an increase of about two millions in each period of ten years.

From 1831 to 1841 the population increased 14 per cent.; in the same period the number of priests was increased 25 per cent., or, in nearly double the proportion.

During the ten following years the population increased 13 per cent., the number of priests 45 per cent.

Lastly, from 1851 to 1861, while the population increased 12 per cent., the number of priests has augmented by nearly 37·67 per cent.

We see, therefore, that, as the population increases, the number of our priests has grown in a double and even triple proportion.

I will now give you some exact figures, which will better enable you to judge of the consoling extension of the Catholic Church in England.

In 1830 we numbered only 434 priests for the

whole of England. We have now 1242, that is, three times as many, within sixty. The number of our churches, which was then only 410, now amounts to 872. From 16 convents, which we possessed in 1830, we have risen in 1863 to 162. Lastly, while in 1830 no house of religious men existed there, in 1850 there were 11, and their number at present amounts to 53.

Allow me now to say a few words concerning that vast city, over which I have received the un-merited honour of being placed by the Holy See as Archbishop, and the true condition of which I have, therefore, the best means of ascertaining.

At first sight, it might be supposed that the progress of Catholicity would be most strikingly manifested in London. Such, however, gentlemen, is not the case. For there we meet with obstacles of which you could hardly form an idea. London is not only the principal centre of the industrial activity of the country, but it is the seat and focus of those most powerful and varied associations, whose great end is to oppose Catholic progress. There it is that all the influence of the Court, the Anglican aristocracy, a wealthy national hierarchy, and the leading press, are arrayed in powerful coalition against our holy religion. In the metropolis

are held those periodical meetings, occupying one
entire month, at which the most eloquent religious
orators are permitted, or rather encouraged, to pour
forth their unchecked bitterness against the Church,
till the place of their meeting, Exeter Hall, has
become an epithet, signifying anti-Catholic feeling
and violence. *There* is a command of almost unlimited wealth lavished to draw our poor children
from our schools and institutions, and to entice
away the poor from their fidelity to their Catholic
pastors and their faith.

At the same time, there is no city, perhaps, in the
world in which the mere *material* obstacles to the
outward expansion of the Church are so formidable
as in London. Thus, to speak only of the acquisi-
tion of land for the building of churches, chapels,
&c., I will state one fact, which would seem
incredible but for its having been mentioned before
parliament by a minister of State :—A small parcel
of land, about three quarters of an acre, situated not
in an aristocratical part of the town, but in one of
its commercial centres, near St. Paul's Cathedral,
was sold at the fabulous price of £180,000.

No, gentlemen, it is not to London that one
must go to contemplate the visible and material
growth of Catholicity in England. If you would

fully appreciate it, you must go beyond the limits of
the capital.   You will find in other dioceses of the
country, beautiful churches, magnificent colleges,
and convents, which would bear to stand, in Belgium, side by side even with your own noble religious edifices.   This is an acknowledgment which I
am glad to make, to the honour of my dear brethren
of the English Episcopate, far more worthy than
myself of the high mission to which they consecrate
themselves with so much zeal, devotedness, and
self-denial.   And if I desired to rejoice the heart of
a Catholic stranger by monumental proofs of the
progress of the faith in England, I would take him
at once to St. Cuthbert's College, near Durham, or
St. Mary's, near Birmingham, to the beautiful Priory
of Stone, in the same diocese, to the Orphanage of
Norwood, in the diocese of Southwark, or, indeed,
to a number of other religious foundations, such as
those of the Benedictines, at Belmont and Downside.

Let us not, however, forget to render full justice
to those religious bodies which, conquering every
discouraging obstacle, have succeeded in adorning
London with edifices great and noble in their
design and execution.*

* I will instance the Oblates of St. Charles (secular priests),
the Ladies of Nazareth House, the Sisters of the Good Shepherd

In connexion with this subject I am tempted to relate an anecdote which is full of truthful elegance. The Cathedral of York is, perhaps, the most perfect in grandeur and grace of any in England. All who have seen it acknowledge it to be a monument worthy indeed of the ages of faith. Now, by the side of this splendid Basilica, there stood, till lately, an humble Catholic chapel. The city, being in need of the ground on which it stood, purchased it, and the proceeds of the sale, together with the contributions of the faithful, have enabled the Bishop of Beverley, who, I am glad to say, is present amongst us to-day, to erect in its place a beautiful church, which will certainly contribute much to the progress of religion. It was, indeed, a bold idea, to raise another church almost within the shadow of that overpowering Minster. But, so far from this proximity having bred contemptuous feelings towards the new and yet infant structure, a Protestant judge, not long ago, as he gazed upon this elegant building, observed : " The old Roman Catholic Cathedral must have struck its roots under ground

and of Compassion, the Marist Fathers, the Passionists, the Colletines, the Sisters of Mercy, the Franciscan Nuns of the Third Order, and many others. The Dominicans are now building a church and convent worthy of their noble Order.

and sent up this graceful sapling at so short a distance !"

Yes, gentlemen, the Catholic Church is springing up again ; it had left its tap-root under the religious soil of England, from which new suckers are now shooting upwards; the sap which was believed to be drained out is rising in them once more. The old plant scents again the waters, and revives, endowed with a marvellous fertility.

But I check myself by remembering that I stand before you to tell the whole truth without any concealment or extenuation. We in England have our weak side, our afflictions and our dangers, as well as our consolations, and, shall I say? our triumphs. Our weak side is the education of our children, whom our poverty prevents us from bringing up as we would desire. Oh! how gladly would I lead some of those generous benefactors, who are always ready to help the unfortunate, into those miserable quarters of London, which swarm with the thick and countless multitudes of England's prolatarians ! How deeply would they be stirred to compassion by the sight of these wretched quarters, threaded by narrow, crooked, and loathsome alleys, in which the air can hardly circulate, and where vice and crime shelter themselves so securely, that the very agents of the police scarcely dare attempt to follow them ! I have been obliged of late frequently to pass through these haunts of misery to visit a Belgian community, which a good priest of your country has had the courage to establish there, to instruct and reclaim that wretched population. Well, gentlemen, I have met hundreds of ragged children in those streets, living the life of absolute abandonment, scarcely having ever known their parents, and ignorant, perhaps, of their own names. To this strange form of childhood has been popularly given the picturesque name of the *London Arabs*.

We are doing all we can to gather these poor little outcasts together, and to give them Christian training. The schools in which they are taught, and to which I am at present alluding, are themselves situated in a truly fearful spot, Charles-street, Drury-lane. We owe them in great measure to the zeal of the Fathers of the Oratory. Their cost has been no less than £12,000. The Religious Sisters of St. Andrew, from Tournay, with a devotion truly heroic, have undertaken the care of the girls' school.

For some time past we have had the consolation of seeing increased, by a thousand a-year, the number of children attending our schools for the poor.

But, notwithstanding all the efforts of charity, there must still remain at least 17,000 poor children who attend no school, or only Protestant schools. This is, as you may believe, gentlemen, an unspeakable sorrow, which I share with all the faithful of my diocese. The cure of this evil seems so beyond our strength, that charitable foreigners have made proposals, which I have gladly accepted, for establishing, on the Continent, an association for promoting the education of the poor in London.

Permit me now to give you a glimpse of the progress which Catholicity has made even in London, notwithstanding all the obstacles with which it has to contend.

In 1826 there were in London 48 Catholic priests; in 1851, 113; in 1863, 194 (now above 200). The number of our churches for these three periods respectively amounts to 24, 46, and 102. At the first of these dates there was but one single convent, at the second 9, now there are above 25. Lastly, while, in 1826, religious houses of men, and institutions of Catholic charity had no place in the statistics of the diocese, the first now amount to 15, the second to 34.

These different pious institutions comprehend an hospital served by religious aggregated to the Order of St. John of Jerusalem, for whom a member of parliament, a convert to Catholicism,* has just now erected, at his own expense, a convent and a magnificent church. They comprise also, almshouses for aged men and women, a large asylum of the Good Shepherd, three reformatories for young criminals of both sexes, six or seven orphanages for boys and girls, to which we hope to add, at no long distance of time, an asylum for deserted children.

All this is, in a manner, new, and is a signal proof of the Divine goodness, and of the care with which our Lord watches over His children.

By the side of our ordinary duties we have others to fulfil which hardly exist out of London. We have to provide for the foreign Catholic population which flows thither. In the month of November last I had the happiness of opening a large and beautiful church for German Catholics, served by priests of their nation. A venerable old man was present at the inauguration of this building. Seventy years before he had witnessed, as a Pro-

---

* Sir G. Bowyer. The Holy Father has presented a chalice of massive gold to the new church. The Order of St. John has given a magnificent altar, and the generous founder has enriched it with the most costly vestments and sacred vessels furnished by the Great Exhibition.

testant, the opening of the temple which we had now devoted to Catholic worship. He had then heard his uncle, officiating as the Protestant minister, predict the speedy downfall of papistical superstitions. The clouds of Catholicism were, according to the prediction of this poor blind guide, to disappear before the Protestant light then rising over London !

On the 16th of April of the present year, with the attendance of nearly all our Bishops, we inaugurated another magnificent temple, a true Basilica, copied from that of St. Chrysogonus at Rome, for the use of the Italians in London ; while its spacious crypt serves as a chapel for the Poles, and is served by a priest recommended to me by the Archbishop of Posen. The French have already, it is true, a chapel of their own, served by excellent priests of their own nation ; but it is inconvenient in this respect, that it is at a considerable distance from the part of London which they chiefly occupy. We hope, therefore, before long, to see a church arise nearer to the French quarter, in which they may receive instructions in their own language. The land for this purpose is already purchased.

There is another standard by which to measure the progress of Catholicity in England, concerning which you would, doubtless, desire to be informed, the number of conversions to the faith. This is a subject of great delicacy, on which you will pardon me if I touch but lightly.

At the beginning of the religious movement in England, which has been fitly termed amongst us, the Catholic movement, some public journals took pleasure in announcing the conversions which were wrought. Such information was, doubtless, very consoling to us ; but this very publicity raised, at the same time, a formidable obstacle to conversions. If, as sometimes happens, the conversion was not complete, timid persons were alarmed, or exposed to various kinds of trial and perplexity. Some even turned back, while almost all felt their spiritual joy diminished, by the vexations which publicity in such matters never fails to bring with it. Many were even persecuted on account of their conversion. The custom of publishing matters connected with conversions was, therefore, gradually dropped. Observe, however, that the publicity formerly given to them was not the work of the clergy, who were fully alive to its danger, but often of other imprudent though well-intentioned persons, who, in their zeal, rejoiced to see the number of the faithful increased by the addition of persons distinguished by their social position. Do not suppose, therefore, gentlemen, that because you hear less than you formerly did of conversions, the current of proselytism is stopped. On the contrary, conversions are continually increasing ; they embrace persons of every position, extending, as formerly, even to the highest in the social scale.

That which is to us a special source of joy is, that more conversions now occur among the middle and industrial classes, in the very heart, that is, of those social regions, which, until lately, had comparatively resisted the exertions of the clergy. Not a few students in the professional classes, such as law and medicine, return to the faith of their fathers. I have lately had the happiness of confirming several new converts belonging to the learned professions.

The generosity of our brethren, thus restored to the unity of the Church, is truly magnificent. Suffice it to allude to one of the members of this great assembly,* who, at his own expense, has built a church at Belmont, near Hereford, large enough to serve as the cathedral of an extensive diocese. I will add, also, that the number of churches built, or being built, by converts, amounts to at least forty-two.

* Mr. Wegg Prosser, late M.P.

This shows, gentlemen, that many of our new
fellow-Catholics have been blessed by Providence
with worldly advantages, and seek to enter the
kingdom of heaven, as did the first converts, by
making generous sacrifices of them for the advance‿
ment of true religion.

The second epoch of Catholic progress, of which
I have spoken, dates from the year 1840, when the
Holy See created a new circumscription of Vicariates
Apostolical, increasing their number from four to
eight. This measure produced the happiest effects,
by augmenting the number of centres of episcopal
vigilance and responsibility, and, consequently, of
pastoral activity. At first the new Bishops found
themselves in such destitution of apostolical labourers,
that, being sometimes alone and without the assist
ance of a single priest at their episcopal residences,
they were obliged to fulfil the office of parish priests
themselves. Gradually their zeal, under the influence of an almost miraculous Providence, over-
came all difficulties, and triumphed over every
obstacle. Where was once only a miserable chapel,
we now find one or more beautiful churches ; new
sources of light have been kindled, which cast their
quickening rays upon spots hitherto out of the
reach of Catholic influence. New missions have

been formed and solidly established ;* thanks, in great measure, to the upright and equitable character of our people, which allows us to address them with frankness, and to their naturally serious and religious turn of mind, which leads them to give a favourable reception to the efforts of disinterested zeal.

To all these causes of progress was now added the most important event in the history of English Catholicity, the creation of the Hierarchy, decreed on the 27th of September, 1850, by the great Pontiff, who now so gloriously rules the Church.

You may remember, gentlemen, that when the tidings reached England of this courageous measure, so worthy in all respects of the Holy See, it excited keenest apprehensions. It was supposed to be fraught with, I know not what of danger and hostility to the nation. Violent passions were awakened, and threatening manifestations, unrepressed by authority, burst forth against the new organization. It was assuredly a moment of delusion with our adversaries, and perhaps a critical moment for ourselves. To many it was a subject of fear and

---

* In England what is elsewhere termed a *parish*, is called by Catholics a *mission*. All priests, in fact, bear the name there of Missionary Apostolic.

anxiety, to us all it was a matter of pain and suffering. But, thanks be to God, our countrymen, since that sorrowful period, have made us such noble and touching reparation, that those days of violent excitement are, I can assure you, for ever effaced from the memory of Catholics.

If the multiplication of Vicariates produced remarkable effects on the progress of religion, the establishment of the Hierarchy must necessarily have added to these advantages, if only by the fact that it brought five additional Sees to the aid of those which already existed. Not to weary you with details, I will only state the fact, that wherever a Bishop appears, a true religious oasis is immediately formed around him, and peopled by Catholic institutions.

The great towns of Manchester and Liverpool, so pre-eminently Catholic, thanks to their Bishops, behold spacious and beautiful churches arise, almost daily, in the midst of them. At Northampton and Plymouth, where but lately Catholicity made but little appearance, cathedrals have sprung up, while religious communities are being established both in town and country.

Around Birmingham, and in other towns of its diocese, several large churches, cemeteries, assigned by the municipalities to the exclusive use of Catholics, convents, orphanages, hospitals, and other charitable institutions, have been also founded by Episcopal zeal.

The town of Hereford, the residence of the Bishop of Newport, boasts the Cathedral of Belmont already mentioned, and a monastery of Benedictines, whose young and fervent Prior is present with us in this assembly. It possesses also a beautiful convent of the religious of the Good Shepherd, and an admirable establishment of Sisters of St. Vincent of Paul, occupied, here as in all other places, in a variety of good works.

If I do not review all our dioceses it is for fear of encroaching upon your time. I must name them all if I would enumerate the consoling fruits which they present, and do justice to the illustrious prelates who govern them. I will only say, that I lately spent a few days in the North of Wales, which now forms a portion of the new Bishopric of Shrewsbury, a region once most remote from Catholic influences. Well, in that distant part of the country, where formerly two or three chapels (of which one was private) sufficed to shelter the scanty number of the faithful, we now find a large college of Jesuit Fathers, a very picturesque convent of Capuchins, by the side of a stately church at Pantasaph,* two houses of religious women, one of them from Holland, and seven new *missions*, or parishes, founded in perpetuity.

Besides these multiplications of religious advantages, consequent upon the increase in the number of Bishoprics, the Hierarchy has conferred upon us other benefits, which the simple augmentation of Vicariates Apostolical would never have been able to obtain for us. Such are the germ of the organization of the parochial system by the nomination in certain missions of priests, with the title of *Missionary Rectors*, who cannot be removed at pleasure; the creation of diocesan Chapters in full enjoyment of their canonical rights and privileges, to which the Holy See, preserving, nevertheless, its own right of nomination intact, has generously granted the honourable privilege of submitting the names of three ecclesiastics for its choice, on the vacancy of a See.

But more important still is the power of holding provincial councils, of which three have been already assembled. After three centuries of disorder and persecution, it was necessary to establish a uniform

---

* Built at the expense of Lord Feilding, a convert, who also gave the land for the houses of the Fathers and of the Sisters of Charity at Pantasaph.

system in accordance with canonical arrangements and with the new Hierarchial order. Amongst other measures of great importance, I will only instance that which was decided in our last Synod—the foundation of an ecclesiastical seminary in every diocese.

Allow me now, gentlemen, to give you some information as to what English Catholics have to do, and are still doing, to complete the work of their emancipation, and to fill up the gaps, and supply the imperfections, still remaining in their social position, especially with regard to the necessitous classes, and those who are unable to help themselves.

I have already remarked upon the difficulty, not to say impossibility, of finding adequate means for the education of our poor. Before the organization of the Hierarchy a kind of council had been formed, under the name of the Poor School Committee, to watch over the interests of our poor children. It is composed of three deputies from each diocese, one of whom is a priest, and the other two laymen of high position, and well known for their zeal and religious self-devotion; for, I am happy to say, that these two qualifications, nobility and faith, are to be found united in England no less frequently than in Belgium.

The president of this council has been, up to the present time, a man who is equally venerated by Catholics and respected by Protestants, who is listened to with all deference, even by persons in the highest official position ; a man who, for many years past, has been at the head of all Catholic works of charity, who has but to make an appeal in the name of religion, to rally around him all that is noblest and most intelligent among Catholics; a man who has deserted his comfortable country home to live in the metropolis, in order that he may be better able to labour for the poor ; a man, in short, who not only by reason of his virtues, but by reason of the advanced age which, for the benefit of religion and charity, Divine Providence has permitted him to attain,* I may venture to place by the side of the venerable man and irreproachable judge, who presides over this assembly.†

Our Poor School Committee has a twofold office: the first consists in the distribution of the gifts and alms collected on a certain day in all the churches of England on behalf of its work. This distribution is made amongst all the schools which stand in

* The Honourable Charles Langdale.

† The Baron de Gerlache, supreme Judge of the Court of Cassation.

need of assistance, with consummate impartiality, judgment, and tact. There has never been a complaint or a remonstrance on the subject of a partition so delicate, and at times so difficult to manage. The meeting for this purpose takes place in London after Easter, at the same time with that of the Bishops of England, and no dissension has ever arisen to disturb the harmony which prevails between these two bodies.

But the Poor School Committee has a higher mission, and one still more important than that of which I have just spoken. It is recognized by government as the official organ of Catholics in all matters relating to the education of the poor. By its intervention, we have negociated with the government, and obtained the advantages which I am about to enumerate.

I. A separate allotment of the funds granted by parliament during the last fifteen years for educational purposes, in favour of schools exclusively Catholic. During this period our schools have received, as their legitimate shares of these funds, a sum total of £239,757, partly for the construction, and partly for the maintenance, of poor schools. Besides this, within the course of eight years, the Privy Council, which is entrusted with the administration of the funds devoted to education, has granted £21,543 to Catholic normal schools for both sexes.

The total amount of grants to Catholic schools obtained by our committee is £268,062.

II. A simple and uniform arrangement, by which the land and building allotted to any poor school are secured to it in perpetuity, and guaranteed against any legal difficulty or interference.

III. The direction of the schools :—Each school is placed under the superintendence of a local committee of Catholics, the president of which is the missionary priest. He is the sole judge of all matters of moral order, or affecting the conduct, instruction, or direction of the school. In case of any difference arising in the council the appeal is to the Bishop of the diocese.

IV. Inspection.—Schools which receive assistance from government are subject to periodical inspection. In our schools, however, this inspection can only be entrusted to Catholic inspectors, approved by the Bishops, and recommended by the Poor School Committee. They are salaried by government, which also defrays the expenses of their journeys.

Such are the concessions granted to Catholics with regard to their poor schools ; they are due, in great measure, to the perseverance of Catholics, both ecclesiastics and laymen acting together with common zeal and in perfect accordance.

I will unite under one head two separate institutions which are intimately related to each other, *Reformatory Schools* and *Schools of Industry*.

The former date from 1854. A law passed at that period enacted, that juvenile offenders, condemned to imprisonment, should, after having passed some weeks in prison, complete their term of punishment in a reformatory, *i. e.*, in an establishment recognised and approved by the Secretary of State for the Home Department.

One day, when I was presiding at a charitable meeting, it had just came to my knowledge that Catholics, placed by the police in these establishments, were not only mixed with Protestants, but exposed to the danger of losing their faith, since no religious instruction was given, or even allowed them. Shocked at this intelligence, I engaged, upon the spot, that before another year, Catholics should have a reformatory of their own. This engagement was fulfilled. In the course of that year our good Catholics bestirred themselves ; a separation was obtained between the Catholic and Protestant delinquents, a large house was hired in the neighbourhood of London, and, in a very short space of time, the first Catholic reformatory was established there, under the direction of the Brothers of Mercy from Malines. I take this opportunity of testifying to the excellence of that institution, founded by your own Canon Scheppers.

Similar establishments were successively opened in different parts of the country, so that we have three for children of each sex.

In 1857 the benefits of this system were extended to children unconvicted of any crime, but abandoned, *i. e.*, without home, or shelter, or parental care, who are found by the police in the streets, and often associated with well-known malefactors. Without obliging them to pass through a prison, which might impress upon them an indelible stigma, the police magistrate sends them to an *industrial school*, recognised by the Secretary of State, for a fixed period, according to their age. It was necessary to provide for this new order of wants, and we set ourselves to do so with all the zeal of which we were capable.

I began my part by purchasing a house, on freehold ground, close to my little country residence in the neighbourhood of London. I have since made considerable additions to it; and this new Catholic industrial school is managed by my secretary, Canon

C

Searle, and by the zealous priest of the mission. We have now 70 boys in it. These useful institutions have since multiplied, and we have now three for boys and as many for girls.

At first some magistrates, for want of information, persisted, notwithstanding the instructions of the Secretary of State, in sending our children to Protestant institutions ; but they have gradually become more alive to the conditions of the case, and have changed their practice.

The members of the Conferences of St. Vincent of Paul also watch closely over their decisions, and are often able to rescue these poor little derelicts from the illegal penalty of the loss of their faith.   I may add, that the Inspector of Prisons is strictly forbidden, when he visits these establishments, to address any question to the children on the subject of religion.

A fourth (perhaps more) of the British army is composed of Irish Catholics, yet no steps had ever been taken to provide for the exercise of their religion, or to give them the benefit of Catholic chaplains.   The law had provided for the army none but Anglican ministers ; but it has at last come to be understood that piety does not stand in the way of valour, and that soldiers who go to confession fight none the less bravely than those who do not.

When the Crimean war broke out, the assistance of some priests was asked to accompany the troops ; and several young and admirable ecclesiastics, of whom some have left their bones in the cemeteries of that distant land, immediately offered themselves, and soon gained the esteem of the officers, and the love of the soldiers entrusted to their pious care.

But these extempore chaplains had no recognised official position, so that their relations and their correspondence with the war office, or the staff of the army, necessarily passed through the hands of the Protestant chaplain-in-chief, a humiliating position for these disinterested and devoted men.

In the month of June, 1858, General Peel put an end to this vexatious inequality. A body of Catholic chaplains was nominated on an equality in all respects with the Protestant, having rank, promotion, salaries, and retiring pensions, precisely similar to theirs. Their number, according to the official report of the 1st of June, 1862, amounted to eighteen, to which we must add sixty-three assistant-chaplains or priests, attached to the troops in their barracks, in all eighty-one, receiving from government £5,921.

The first time that a proposal was made to Parlia-

ment to take similar measures in behalf of Catholic
sailors on board the fleet, it was received with con-
tempt, almost with indignation. But on this point,
also, time and perseverance have wrought their effect
upon the minds of our people. The government
carried without opposition, in the budget, the sum
necessary to repair this injustice. In each of our
three great harbours a vessel is moored, prepared
for Catholic worship, with a chaplain, having a salary
of £125, specially appointed to the spiritual care of
the Catholic sailors.

The men of war, in the neighbouring ports, are
obliged to send them on Sunday to hear Mass on
board these ships, and they are thereby dispensed
from the hard necessity of attending the Protestant
service.

Two important matters still occupy our attention,
of which one may be considered as already arranged,
and the other on the way to a settlement. I mean
the deplorable and iniquitous position of Catholics
in our prisons and workhouses. I will say a few
words on both these points.

In England there are two principal classes of
prisons. There are seven set apart for the deten-
tion of prisoners undergoing their punishment;
these are under the jurisdiction of the Secretary of

State. The country and borough gaols are under the management of the local justices of the peace.

Besides the prisons, we have large and numerous establishments in England, called *Union Workhouses.* These are new institutions, belonging to several parishes, associated together to maintain, by means of local taxes, persons, who, from sickness or want of employment, are unable to earn their bread. Once shut up in either, no Catholic could obtain assistance of a priest, without a formal request made as often as his aid was desired. At the same time, the Protestant chaplain had free access daily to the Catholic prisoner, even in his cell, where the system of solitary confinement prevails. The wicked and hardened naturally cared not to make a petition, which was usually received with a bad grace, and which sometimes exposed them to persecution. They were often made to feel the difference between Catholics and Protestants.

As to the poor orphan children who were sent to the workhouse, when once within its doors, there was no more thought of Catholicity for them. The authorities refused even to give the names of these unfortunate little creatures to the priest, when he inquired for them ; they denied their existence, and

sent them to a great distance in the country, the
better to secure their perversion.

These evils were common to these two classes:—
the *vineti in mendicitate et ferro,* those " in bonds
for destitution or crime,"—in the workhouse and
the prison,—were confounded together in the same
injustice. The measure was full ; and liberal and
honourable Catholics could no longer, without being
wanting to their duty and their conscience, tolerate
an iniquity which cried to heaven for vengeance.

In 1853 Mr. Lucas spoke of it with strong emotion in the House of Commons. One of the liberal
ministry replied by an assertion, which was wholly
inaccurate, that the Catholic Ecclesiastical Authorities made no complaint of the existing state of
things, and that no change was required.

Our Catholics, however, did not lose courage, but
continued their energetic efforts with the ministry.
At the same time, with their venerable Nestor at
their head, they assembled, on the 8th of June,
1859, in the great St. James's Hall, in London,
forming the most numerous and imposing meeting
of Catholics which had ever taken place, as to
ability, social position, enthusiasm, and perfect
unity of sentiment. They did not come together,
as on former occasions, to vindicate their right as

Catholic citizens to a place in the two Houses of Parliament. No, it was to obtain for the most miserable of their fellow-Catholics, for criminals and paupers, those spiritual consolations which religion alone can afford. Thank God! faith and charity, far more than politics, awaken, excite, and set in motion now-a-days the Catholic spirit in England.

It is but justice to remark that, during the short administration of Lord Derby, the head of the Tory party in 1858, Catholics received encouraging replies to their remonstrances on the abuses and acts of oppression, proved against the establishments of which I have been speaking.

When the Conservative Cabinet was dissolved, the new minister, Lord Palmerston, found, according to custom in use amongst us, two memoranda left by the outgoing ministers, Packington and Estcourt, proving the good intentions of the previous government with regard to Catholics in the navy, and those confined in prisons and workhouses; in consequence of commissions confided to the two ministers above mentioned, by the chief of their cabinet.

The change of ministry took place in the month of May, 1859, and on the 20th of June following a numerous deputation of Catholics was received by the Premier, now re-established in his former position, to lay before him those great questions which, with good reason, filled and agitated the minds of the faithful.

We must here separate the grievances, the redress of which we seek, because of the different effects produced by our remonstrances. Suffice it to say, that the deputation presented to Lord Palmerston a memorial carefully drawn up, which had received the assent of the great assembly, to which I have alluded. This memorial contained six demands, which, if granted, would give full and entire satisfaction to Catholics on all the points at issue.

In 1861 a Catholic committee was formed in London, to undertake the cause of the prisoners with the government, and, in the House of Commons, Lord Edward Howard, having proposed a measure to the same end, withdrew it on a promise made by the minister that he would take the matter seriously in hand.

Accordingly, in the following year, Lord Palmerston proposed, in the budget, a sum of £550 to be divided amongst the Catholic chaplains of seven penal prisons, dependant upon government, in which Catholics were thenceforward placed on the same footing with Protestants. The subsidy was granted, and amounts exactly to the same sum which had been proposed to the House by the same minister in 1854, and which was then rejected.

As to the gaols in towns and counties, the government was unable, from lack of authority, to act in the same effectual way ; but, after much discussion, a law was obtained, empowering the local magistrates to appoint a salaried Catholic chaplain to a prison, whenever they should judge the number of Catholic inmates sufficient, or even to indemnify a priest who should consent to visit them freely ; with authority, in both cases, to defray the expense thus incurred from the county rates, which had not hitherto been allowed.

This law has passed the legislature during the course of the present year. It remains to be seen whether it will be sufficient, or whether it ought to be rendered obligatory.* It at least excludes all relations between the Protestant minister and the Catholic prisoners, unless by their expressed desire.

On the workhouse question, the debate is not yet terminated, but we have little fear of the result.

* While this Address is being prepared for the press, the experiment has been tried. It has had favourable results at Worcester, Liverpool, and partly at Wakefield. It has failed in Middlesex, and some other places.

To overcome the obstacles still raised by our adversaries, it seemed necessary to form, in 1860, a Catholic committee in London, to superintend and direct this matter.

A young but able and devoted ecclesiastic has contributed, with great zeal, prudence, and skill, to the success of this holy cause. As secretary of the committee he has borne the hardest burthen of its labours, having made it his peculiar care to publish a monthly report devoted to the cause of our unfortunate brethren.

To this same priest, the Canon Morris, we owe, also, the direction of the parliamentary inquiry, which we boldly demanded. The facts, on which we grounded our remonstrances, were denied ; we were told that Catholics were perfectly well-treated, and subjected to no kind of injustice in the unions. The commission of inquiry was granted to us in 1861. The majority was composed of Protestants, chosen from all the different parties in the House, to whom were added three Catholics. Witnesses were heard on both sides. The proofs of oppression and injustice were glaring, the defence pitiable.

The report to the House has been drawn up. Peculiar circumstances have hitherto prevented its publication, but we have every reason to believe that it is entirely favourable to us, and that the measures which it will suggest will put an end to the last of our just grievances.

Gentlemen, these are certainly not great facts worthy to attract the attention of the world, or calculated to shed new lustre on the Church; but they testify, as it seems to me, to the zeal and perseverance which English Catholics bring to the vindication and defence of their religious liberties ; and it is enough for me that, on this plea, they will obtain your sympathy and your prayers.

But, before I pass on to the second part of my subject, permit me to discharge a debt which weighs upon my heart.

I return thanks, in the name of all the Bishops of our Hierarchy, to my Lords the Prelates of the Belgian Episcopate, for the inestimable services which they have rendered us, and which have contributed so largely to the progress of which I have been speaking.

An English seminary has been recently founded at Bruges by the generosity of an English convert. This establishment is already flourishing under the direction of Belgian Superiors ; and there, besides the student of our own nation, several Belgians are preparing themselves for the exercise of their

ministry in England. If we are to calculate in anti-
cipation their services, by those already rendered to
us by their zealous countrymen, who have volun-
tarily preceded them, we may rejoice beforehand in
their full success.

The prosperity of such an establishment must
always depend, in great measure, upon the benevo-
lent protection of the Bishop who superintends it.
Alas! gentlemen, I avail myself, with real sorrow, of
the sad circumstance which permits me to speak
with greater freedom than I could have ventured to
do, but for the severe illness which deprives us of
his presence here, of that distinguished Prelate, who
is one of the ornaments, not only of Belgium, but of
the whole Church. Others may praise him for his
varied and profound erudition, his administrative
activity, or even his Christian and Episcopal virtues.
I must content myself with offering to him, in the
midst of his sufferings (which may God relieve !)
the tribute of the deep and lively gratitude of English Catholics for his paternal goodness to one humble college, and its young students who are learning
there, to imitate the virtues of the excellent priests
who surround and direct them.

I have already mentioned, with the praise which
they deserve, the Brothers of Mercy of Malines, who

direct most admirably two large institutions in my diocese. We have also seven communities of religious women of Belgian origin, who aid us by their works and their prayers. God alone can recompense their charity and their self-devotion.

Indeed, to Him alone do we owe all. You, gentlemen, have preserved, and have only to continue the great and noble works of your fathers. For us, everything has to be created: and the only Creator is God.

Gentlemen, I have now reached the second part of my Address; and I feel that it is by far the most difficult and the most delicate. I have to lay before you the means which have been employed by the Catholics of England, and, with God's blessing, successfully, to obtain the concessions justly claimed by them.* I have shown you that the efforts to obtain some of these have lasted, without intermission, for ten years before being crowned with success; and I should not be doing justice to my theme if I did not communicate to you

---

* There were seven enumerated in the first part: 1st, separate education of Catholic poor children; 2nd, separate reformatories; 3rd, similar industrial schools for children in danger; 4th, chaplains for the army; 5th, for the navy; 6th, prison chaplains; and, 7th, the same for workhouses.

the manner in which such exertions have been made.

First, let me observe, that we are in a different position from you. We have not had ours to choose ; we have not had the responsibility of selecting our own form of government. Divine Providence has done all this for us. We find ourselves under the constitutional form of govern-ment, which has existed in our country for cen-turies, and gladly accept it; we throw ourselves loyally into its duties and principles, and employ, energetically, those means and instruments which it places at our command, for obtaining the redress of wrongs continued, and the concession of rights withheld.

The Catholics of England expect no favours, and do not ask for them. Justice, as done to their fellow-citizens, is all they demand. Were any one to come to them, as did the prophet to the Suna-mite, and offer to obtain their just petitions through favour, were he to say, " Have you any affair about which you would wish me to speak to the highest authority in the realm, or shall I use my influence at the War Department, in the matter of your military chaplains?" I believe they would answer, with that wise and good woman, " I dwell in the midst of my people."* That is, I require and desire no favours; I am one of the nation; I am satisfied to be like any of my fellow-subjects, treated on a footing of perfect equality with them.

And this is, and has been, the language and the sentiment of our Catholics in England; " You may have knocked off our fetters, but while the ring, by which they were fastened, still remains round our ankles or wrists, we cannot rest satisfied. Our Protestant fellow-subjects bear no such remnant of old oppression, which would gall even if it did not hold captive." They have made up their minds that, within the limits of the constitution, they must not rest till they have gained this equality. And how?

We know of only one way under our form of government. In a constitutional monarchy we recognize only two powers in intimate relation; the crown and the people represented in its two houses. One can recognize no third estate, no intermediate power.

A ministry is the organ of communication between these two essential powers. It bears from the higher

* " Numquid habes negotium, et vis ut loquar regi, sive principi militiæ? Quæ respondit; in medio populi mei habito."—4 Reg. iv.

to the lower the resolutions emanating from the supreme prerogatives invested in it; it carries up from the lower to the higher its wishes, its desires, its respectful suggestions, to obtain the final sanction of the throne.

The moment this mechanism fails in its object; so soon as the measure which, through its responsible agency, the royal authority has sent for deliberation to its assembled councillors, is rejected by them; or the determinations of these are such, that it cannot consistently, with its avowed principles, hold itself responsible for them to the crown, it is deranged in its organic action, and must be either replaced or repaired. But, as a power in itself, it is no recognized element of constitutional government. And particularly we can recognize in it no distinct power, as having right or might to perpetuate old abuses, or create them for the future.

It is, then, to the Constitutional Powers of the State that the Catholics of England address themselves. But here how different is their condition from yours! You form the nation. Your whole electoral body is Catholic. Your candidates are for the most part Catholics. Your chambers are mainly composed of members of your own religion.

In England it is the opposite way. The Catholics

there form a small minority, scattered thinly over the country, except in a few parts, and in some large towns. Out of these their power and influence as electors is almost null. In fact, England sends only one Catholic to the House of Commons. Still, the inequality of the electoral contest, and the smallness of their chances, do not make the Catholics despair. There are places where their number is totally insufficient to secure a seat for one of themselves; but, where there are several candidates, they may be able, if united, to make one or the other side of the balance prevail, and seat a member who professes just views, and, at any rate, not hostile intentions.

It is only lately that Catholics have learnt their power, even in large constituencies, and have given some startling proofs of it. I will illustrate this by allusion to a case which occurred at our last election. A candidate in a considerable town came before the electors on liberal principles, and was surprised to find himself rejected by the preponderance of Catholic votes, which turned the scale. He was informed that the motive for this conduct was his having exceeded even the liberty accorded to an advocate, in a cause which he had pleaded against a Catholic bishop, in order to excite the religious prejudice of a jury. He was told that he would meet with the same determined and organized opposition in another place where he intended to try his chance. This was the case. So, having to stand for the very place where that bishop lived, he called upon him, and made his peace.

I will mention another instance, to show what very limited influence may accomplish. In a small borough, a candidate came forward, canvassing on an anti-Catholic principle, as the great promoter of a bill to harass religious houses. He expected, no doubt, to carry all the Protestant, and, particularly, the Dissenting interest. There was only one Catholic voter of any position in the town, and he the only one of his family. But he brought his fellow-townsmen together, and convinced them, from the candidate's antecedents, that, though an enemy to Catholics, he was no friend to Dissenters, and he lost his election.

These examples may show how Catholics strive to avail themselves of the very small electoral power which they possess in England. It has been sufficient, first, to exclude a certain number of adverse, or, at least, more than ordinarily prejudiced members from the House of Commons, and to make their influence, in divided and nearly balanced constituencies, worth estimating in their calculations by the great political parties of the country.

It is evident that, were we to rely on our power
in influencing parliamentary votes through our action
on constituencies or on elections, in order to obtain
what we are entitled to, our chances would be indeed
extremely small. We have, therefore, to put our
trust in more powerful influences. First, we have
an unbounded confidence in the justice of our cause.
Those who have undertaken it, in every instance,
can have no selfish or even personal interest in it.
Poor children, youthful delinquents, soldiers, sailors,
and the inmates of prisons and workhouses, belong
not to their own class, or even to those classes with
whom they are brought habitually into contact. They
are removed from them by many intermediate
layers in society. Nothing but a deep, religious
sense of justice can urge them to give up time, energy,
and influence to the succour and alleviation of the
most destitute and helpless.

Now, the cause of all such is the cause of the
God of justice and of power. And when the depri-
vation of rights or the exercise of oppression is the
consequence, at least accidental, of their conscien-
tious adhesion to the Catholic religion, it is not
wonderful that we should feel it an absolute duty
to exert all our means in their favour. " Thrice is

he armed," says "the greatest of our poets, " who hath his quarrel just."

Hence, our full conviction of the justice of our demands is equivalent to an unlimited confidence in the Divine justice, that, if we persevere in our efforts, sooner or later we shall succeed. This is our first, our firmest, and our surest trust.

Then we have an unbounded confidence in the ultimate justice of our fellow-countrymen. We know that individuals may have their minds thoroughly penetrated with prejudices from early education, and later influences, particularly from the press. But experience has proved that at the bottom, buried beneath this confused heap of false, and even absurd convictions, there is a powerful sense of justice, which, if properly evoked, will make its way through these erroneous teachings, and, standing above them, will tread them under foot.

But as we cannot address each individual conscience, we feel an equal confidence, if, true to constitutional principles, we appeal to the general *resultant* of their forces through their representation in parliament. Hence, every one of the important concessions which I have mentioned, as obtained by Catholics, has passed through this channel, whether by special Act or admission in the estimates ; in fact, have been awarded by the nation, gradually, steadily, and perseverently convinced of the justice of each claim. It has not been a struggle of party, to which we were unequal : it has been the contest of patient confidence ; at first, once and again losing, then slowly gaining, till at last the justice of our demands has been acknowledged. Then, perhaps, have come partial concessions, then greater; till we have either obtained, or feel sure of obtaining, all that we desire.

We have little or no command of the periodical press ; scarcely any facilities for addressing large meetings ; hardly personal weight in guiding public feeling. But we have a few zealous and sincere advocates in both Houses of Parliament, who appeal there to the national conscience, and, by degrees, succeed in rousing it. We have the unlimited power of petitioning ; and this, when employed by large united multitudes, carries great weight. But, more particularly, on important and contested points we have the still more valuable right of asking for a Special Committee of either House, composed of members belonging to every party, who may call before them or accept the evidence of voluntary witnesses on both sides, together with documentary corroborations ; and then report to the House their judgment on the whole evidence, printed with the Committee's recommendation.

To this, as I mentioned, we had recourse in the very grave question of relief to Catholic inmates of workhouses. An impartially selected Committee of the Commons sat for months, and carefully examined many witnesses. The real merits of the case were thus brought before the nation in the most constitutional form. As an illustration of the utility of this proceeding, and readiness to acknowledge just claims, though we need expect no favour, I may cite the confession of one member of the Committee, who mentioned to a friend that he entered upon it under the persuasion that we had nothing to complain of in this matter ; but that the evidence brought before him had convinced him that our poor were suffering great oppression, and that he would do all in his power to have justice done us.

In this change of feeling we put immense trust. This gentleman is but the type of many ; these many constitute a strong power, sure to grow into an honest majority. And so, although owing, I believe, to special reasons, which it is not necessary to detail, the Report of the Committee has not been laid before the House, we look forward to its results with calm confidence in public justice.

There is one instance of the security of our reliance on the good faith and justice of our fellow-countrymen, which I am sure will gratify your feelings. Some years ago, a most gratuitous attempt was made, and steadily pursued by members of our parliament, to interfere with the liberty of the religious life. Not only were measures proposed which would throw obstacles in the way of entering into religious houses, but domiciliary visits, both unbecoming in themselves, and totally at variance with English usage and feelings, were proposed to be made, almost at discretion, to the chosen retreats from the world of ladies exclusively, or in great part, belonging to the highest and most honoured families in England.

There were found many to applaud, and some to second this unworthy proposal, which filled all Catholics with sorrow, shame, and indignation. But Providence brought about its own solution, through the justice of our public national feeling. The question was decided, not on the floor of the House of Commons, but on the shores of the Chersonesus, on the scarp of the Redan, with carbine on the arm, and sword in the right hand.

The Crimean war broke out, and it was wisely considered that every comfort should be provided for
the poor soldier, sick or wounded.

The demand now was : " *Mulierem fortem quis
inveniet ?*"—" Who will find us the courageous
woman ?"*—the woman who is ready to brave the
sea and its storms—perhaps fever and pestilence ;
who does not fear to abandon her native land, and
be an exile among strangers and heathens ; still
more to exchange her peaceful and sacred home
for the life of the camp, in company often with a
rude, or an unthinking, soldiery ?   And the Catholic
Church replied : I will—not seek or find one such,
but give, for I already possess many.   The calm, un-
impassioned, and retired religious ladies, so much
misunderstood, are ready at once to start for the seat
of discomfort and of danger, to nurse and solace
our suffering soldiers.

And so they went cheerfully from Ireland and
from England, and did their work bravely; and,
when they returned, instead of meeting any wish to
pluck their consecrated veils from their heads, they
found the readiness to fasten on them the medal,
equally awarded to the soldier and the nun—a
testimonial that the courage of the one on the

* Prov. xxxi. 10.

battle-field is rivalled by the other's in the field of charity. Since, then, we have had no more attempts to interfere with ladies who have proved themselves to be as patriotic as they are virtuous.

This reliance on the justice, not of a party, but of the country, necessarily makes the course of action pursued by the Catholic body in England independent of temporary circumstances. They do not wait for what might be considered propitious moments, or periods of ministerial crisis. Their progress must be slow ; one claim must be made at a time, that it may be calmly and leisurely enforced ; and then another must succeed, till all shall have been favourably exhausted. Even the most just takes a long time to reach the surface of public opinion.

The pursuit of one of the most important of our demands has traversed three ministries without deviating in its course, and, I am happy to add, has traversed them successfully.

Considering, in this manner, any cause of charity and religion as out of the sphere of mere political opinions, it is not wonderful that English Catholics should make their prosecution of such sacred purposes independent of any party differences within themselves.

And here I feel the importance of expressing my sentiments with all candour and plainness. · You have granted complete liberty of speech to all who have addressed you ; you must have granted equal liberty of thought to all who have listened. There is no *solidarity* of sentiment amongst us here. No one is bound to the theories, however eloquently as to ideas, however elegantly in phrase, they may have been delivered. On the contrary, the more brilliantly such theories are propounded, the more persuasive or seducive the treatment of them may be, the closer guard we must place over our minds, lest we be carried away from our steady principles. And none will more respect this independence of opinion and of speech than those who have most strongly advocated perfect liberty. I have only to speak of England ;—and I feel confident that the attempt to force the Catholics there into one exclusive and extreme political view, or to make our obtaining of redress or of right dependent on all holding the same principles beyond those of constitutional unanimity, would prove not only dangerous but fatal to our purposes.

In our body there exist all possible shades of political opinions. We have men professing the most decided conservative principles ; we have others who push their liberal ideas as far as is consistent with moral and social maxims. But, when a question of justice arises, there is no inquiry made concerning these differences. All unite as in one common cause, and concur in one uniform course of action. So far, with the Divine blessing, we have succeeded; and I trust that, when the Church has need of our services, especially on behalf of her poor, the same unanimity will prevail, without any admixture of political contention.

Gentlemen, it is not for the weak to encourage the strong. We are but few, you are many; we are a fragment of the population, you are the nation. Yet, one has heard repeatedly, almost from every speaker, that the Catholics of Belgium are suffering wrong; are deprived year by year of fresh rights; are trodden down and oppressed. I cannot but ask, by whom?

Not by the violence of any foreign invasion, against which you have not even thought of sharpening your swords.

Not by the power of the Crown: of that dynasty which you have so heartily adopted, and which has given to your nation a king as attached and devoted to it as if it had been his own country; a queen, the memory of whose virtues is yet embalmed in the hearts of all her subjects ; and a family of princes, who, body and heart, by birth as well as by affection, are entirely Belgian.

Is it, then, by the use of the constitutional power of the people that you are wronged and oppressed ? But *you* are the people, and surely can command the direction of your own power. To be cast down, assaulted, wounded, and have your political life extinguished by your own arm—why this is suicide— the only suicide of which a nation is capable.

Gentlemen, the arms of Belgium display a beautiful motto : " *L'union fait la force.*"—" Union makes strength." It represents to us various component elements, each weak, if alone; but, when closely united, capable of resisting much violence and adverse strength.

The Church has one more beautiful still, but which cannot be assumed by any earthly principality, for it describes a characteristic which can only be communicated from above. " *Union,*" she says to you, " constitutes *your* strength : UNITY makes mine"—the unity of that rock, which no endless action of time can wear away, no fury of the infernal tempests overthrow or shake. As Belgians, be

UNITED in loyalty, fidelity, and community of interests ; as Catholics, be ONE in faith, in charity, in zeal, and in adhesion to the centre of unity: and you will carry all your just claims, and attain all your sacred ends.

THE END.

J. MOORE, Printer, 2, Crampton-quay, Dublin.